Shell Kepler
MAKE FASHION MAGIC

To Lovely Donna
"Just Because"
Sandra de
02·04·03

Oxmoor House

Shell Kepler
MAKE FASHION MAGIC

with Danica d'Hondt

If it's true that people live on through memories, then my mother comes to visit every day.

Shell Kepler MAKE FASHION MAGIC

Editor-in-Chief: Nancy Fitzpatrick Wyatt
Senior Homes Editor: Mary Kay Culpepper
Senior Editor, Editorial Services: Olivia Kindig Wells
Art Director: James Boone

Editors: Ann Marie Harvey, Lelia Gray Neil
Assistant Editor: Adrienne E. Short
Editorial Assistant: Laura A. Fredericks
Associate Art Director: Cynthia Rose Cooper
Copy Editor: L. Amanda Owens
Photographer: Ralph Anderson
Photo Stylist: Virginia Cravens
Illustrator: Kelly Davis
Production and Distribution Director: Phillip Lee
Associate Production Manager: Vanessa Cobbs Richardson
Production Assistant: Valerie L. Heard
Publishing Systems Administrator: Rick Tucker

Contents

Spring
page 10

Summer
page 42

Fall
page 72

Winter
page 98

Foreword

It all began with a mother's dream for her daughter.

WHEN SHELL KEPLER WAS FOUR YEARS OLD, her mother, Charlotte Ann, taught her to sew and to design her own clothes. Charlotte Ann hoped her daughter would become a fashion designer someday. But Shell had another dream: to be an actress.

After moving to California from Tennessee at age 10, Shell worked with her mother in the family flower shop until her mother's death a few years later. After Shell recovered from this stunning loss, she pursued acting in earnest.

Seventeen years ago, Shell joined the cast of ABC-TV's "General Hospital" as the lovably dizzy Nurse Amy Vining, winning the part over more than two hundred other candidates. With her signature role on one of television's most enduring daytime dramas, Shell became part of a pop culture phenomenon.

Even after Shell fulfilled her acting ambitions, she continued to make and to embellish her clothes. People starting noticing what Shell calls her California Belle style. Renowned Beverly Hills retailer Fred Hayman was so impressed with her designs that he personally requested a selection for his store on Rodeo Drive. Popular stores such as J.C. Penney and Broadway also began selling her clothes.

Shell developed her most famous line of women's wear—the Lacy Afternoon label— seven years ago for Home Shopping Network. Shell designs these affordable clothes with as much thought, effort, and attention to detail as any couturier. She selects every fabric and button that defines her designs. The seven new collections she unveils each year are soft and romantic and flatter a variety of figures.

There are thousands of Lacy Afternoon fans around the country who travel at their own expense to attend Shell's public appearances. The "Lacy Ladies" collect and trade pieces of the line and chat on-line about Shell and her latest designs. They always call Home Shopping Network when Shell is on the air, and many buy every Lacy Afternoon piece offered.

Part of what inspires such devotion is Shell's contention that high-quality fashion should be accessible to every woman. Here is a chance to make an original Shell Kepler design for yourself. And while some people may recognize her style as your inspiration, the result will nonetheless be your own exclusive creation.

In the words of one of the Lacy Ladies, "Shell shows you that you, too, can make fashion into wearable art."

It's a sentiment Shell's mother would have been proud of.

Introduction

When I was a little girl, my mother always made my clothes. All except one time.

I THINK I WAS SEVEN. You see, we were going to an annual country picnic that was at a park on the lake. Not only was there barbecue and bingo, but there was also The Boy, who was eleven. He had been at the picnic the year before, and it was rumored that he'd be there again. I had sensed that he was uncomfortable with our age difference, so I knew I had to look more mature. I insisted that my mother and I shop for something special. What Mom thought would be a loving, bonding stroll down the avenues—a kind of mother-daughter experience—turned out to be *A Nightmare on Elm Street*, a shop-till-you-drop scene.

We scoured the malls and bombarded the boutiques, but nothing was quite right, which indicated my high maintenance factor even then. Everything was either too big, too little, or just too much money. At that point, my mother was convinced that making "Glinda's" dress with "Dorothy's" slippers or the outfit the lady wears on that "Jeannie" show ("Oh, come on, Mom, you know the one....") would have been easier than enduring this shopping expedition.

Having exhausted all the possibilities (and my mother), we were headed for our final stop: to the drugstore for aspirin for Mom.

Suddenly, from the backseat, I shrieked in her ear, **"Stop the car!"** There it was, right in Miller Brothers' window. This had to be fate. It was a turquoise-with-daisies, puffed-sleeve culotte dress with a sweetheart neckline (slightly décolleté) *and a matching hat!* My mother thought it was cute, and it was on sale, so she let me take it home.

Words can't express how I felt on picnic morning. It had been confirmed that The Boy would be there. I was experiencing an odd combination of feelings. All tingly and light with anticipation, I was still grounded by the confidence of knowing my outfit was daring but understated, chic yet adorable.

Finally, I was on my way! Lying in the back of the station wagon, I traced The Boy's name in the air with my finger. I stirred when my father parked the wagon under a shady tree. Mom, Dad, and my big brother, Freddy, piled out of the car. I adjusted my matching hat. Dad came around to the back to let me out. He opened the tailgate and *voilà!* I was about to debut.

Before I could set one pom-pommed tenny on the ground, I noticed a group of people nearby. They were oohing and aahing over what looked to be my outfit. I started gasping for air. My vision blurred. Was I seeing double? My young life began to pass before my eyes. Then in unison, somewhere off in

the distance, I heard the familiar voices of my family saying, "Uh-oh!" They were trying desperately to pull me back from the white light I was being drawn toward—back to reality. And in reality, my vision was not blurred. I *was* seeing double: two turquoise dresses, two matching hats, two outfits exactly like mine. Standing within the cluster of people were two of the cutest dimple-faced darlings you've ever seen. They couldn't have been a day over three. No longer did my sweetheart neckline look décolleté. I'd been cloned by the itsy-bitsy "Bobbsey Twins." Mortified and numb, I retreated to my sanctuary in the back of the car. I closed the hatch and refused to come out until the sun had set—and The Boy had gone.

To add insult to injury, Freddy spent the entire day hanging out and eating barbecue with his new buddy—The Boy, whose name I have selectively forgotten.

The moral of this story (although I'm sure some of you parents will come up with your own) is *If you don't want someone else wearing it, make it yourself.*

— *Shell Kepler*

Spring

*The heady bouquet of spring is
intoxicating.*

When I think of spring, I think of
what's in the air—the scents of orange
blossoms and honeysuckle, the sounds of
Easter parades and bees. Everything is fresh
and new. From flowers and fashions to butterflies and pollen, it all seems to float by—
especially pollen.

Wistfully looking out the window, wishing the willow were the only thing weeping,
the teary-eyed heroine from a Southern
romance novel is just little ol' me with
spring sniffles, trying not to sneeze.

In-the-Pink Fringed Shawl

Slink this rapturous wrap around your shoulders just once, and you'll find yourself wearing it again and again.

Tint approximately 1¾ yards of white beaded fringe in a pale pink dyebath.

Mix up the dyebath in your washing machine. See pages 122 and 123 for dyeing instructions. Don't agitate the machine because that might damage the beaded fringe. Once the fringe is a color that matches the damask and lace, set it aside to dry. (Remember that the fringe may dye a slightly lighter color.)

Cut a rectangle of pink damask about 1⅔ yards long by 30" wide. Using the damask rectangle as a guide, cut a rectangle from the pink lace. Add ⅜" seam allowances to each.

Pin one rectangle to the other, with right sides together. (You may want to flop the damask to let the prettier side show through when the shawl is worn.) Stitch the rectangles together along the long sides to form a tube. Turn the tube right side out and press the seams.

Hot-glue pink ribbon rosebuds and pink Austrian crystals randomly on the lacy side of the shawl. Be sure to spread your shawl out flat when you do this, since the glue attaches the two pieces of fabric all along the length of the shawl.

Turn the seam allowances at each end of the shawl to the inside and press in place. Top-stitch close to the edges.

Handstitch fringe in place to the damask. (You could also machine-zigzag the fringe by just catching the border of the fringe with the edge of the stitches. There's a risk, though, of breaking the beads in the sewing machine.)

What to Use

Supplies: White beaded fringe, Rose Pink #7 RIT® Dye, pink damask with a nice drape, soft lace in a complementary shade of pink, pink ribbon rosebuds, pink Austrian crystals, thread to match, clear hot-glue sticks

Tools: Tape measure, washing machine, scissors, straight pins, sewing machine, hot-glue gun, needle

Spring air is often chilly on the beach, and this shawl is just enough to keep me comfortable.

True Blue Denim & Damask Vest

As soon as I found these two fabrics, I knew I wanted to combine them with faded blue denim.

Make a tissue paper pattern of the front and back yokes and the center front panels of the vest (your vest may be slightly different, so cover the areas you desire). To do this, lay the garment on a flat surface and pin pieces of tissue paper over the areas you want to cover. Trace a pattern for each piece with a pencil or a ballpoint pen, adding ⅜" seam allowances all around. (You may make a pattern of half the back yoke and place the back center on a fold when you cut out the fabric.) Pin the tissue patterns to the damask and cut them out.

Turn the edges of the damask pieces under ⅜". Pin the seam allowances in place and press. Carefully position the pieces on the vest. Pin them in place. If your vest has conventional buttons, remove them at this point and replace them when you've finished stitching. If your vest has nonremovable studs, mark with a dressmaker's pencil exactly where the studs will be on the damask yoke. With a craft knife, cut slashes in the damask at the marks so that the studs can be worked through. Treat the edges of these slashes with liquid ravel preventer. (You can skip this step if you won't be buttoning your vest.)

Stitch each damask piece in place, stitching close to the edge with a small straight stitch on the sewing machine. Follow the topstitching of the original garment so that it resembles the denim stitching.

To glamorize the studs, hot-glue a blue ribbon rosebud to each one. For the buttons on the pocket flaps, button first and then hot-glue a ribbon rosebud on each stud.

What to Use

Supplies: Denim vest, two complementary damask fabrics in ecru and blue, liquid ravel preventer, thread to match, blue ribbon rosebuds, clear hot-glue sticks

Tools: Tissue paper, straight pins, tracing pencil, scissors, craft knife, sewing machine, hot-glue gun, dressmaker's pencil (optional), ruler (optional)

I don't plan to wear the vest buttoned, so I didn't cut the buttonholes through the damask on the right-hand side of the vest. That way the decorated buttons don't have to be worked through the existing buttonholes.

Sweetheart Apron

Just for the fun of it, I tied bows from pearls-by-the-yard trim and attached them under the roses.

Wear this frothy confection in the kitchen, and you'll look just dishy.

Make a dyebath from Scarlet, Cardinal Red, and Rose Pink. Dye the apron, following the instructions on pages 122 and 123. Hang it to dry.

Make patterns for the bib and the pocket. Pin tissue paper to the apron front. Using a pencil or a ballpoint pen, trace a heart shape over the bib to cover it entirely (refer to the photo for placement and scale). Add a ½" seam allowance on all sides. Then trace the pocket, adding a ½" seam allowance on all sides. Pin the tissue patterns to the brocade and cut them out.

Press under the seam allowances on the heart. Pin the heart in place on the apron bib. Machine-stitch the heart to the apron.

Fold the cut edges of the double-ruffled lace under. Pin the lace to the heart, starting at the bottom of the heart and working your way around. Trim the excess lace. Machine-stitch the lace in place with two rows of stitching.

Press the seam allowances under on the brocade pocket. Using two rows of stitching, machine-stitch the double-ruffled lace to the top edge of the pocket. Pin the pocket to the existing apron pocket, being careful to keep the pocket top edge free from the apron. Machine-stitch close to the edges.

Hot-glue ribbon rosebuds to the lace at regular intervals on the heart and the pocket. And just for the fun of it, tie bows from pearls-by-the-yard trim and attach them to the crevice of the heart and to the left side of the pocket top. Glue large ribbon roses on top of the bows. Add iridescent leaf embellishments under the roses with hot glue.

What to Use

Supplies: White bib-style apron; Scarlet #5, Cardinal Red #9, and Rose Pink #7 RIT Dye; brocade; thread to match; double-ruffled lace; pearls-by-the-yard trim; ribbon roses; iridescent leaf embellishments; clear hot-glue sticks

Tools: Tissue paper, pencil or ballpoint pen, straight pins, scissors, sewing machine, hot-glue gun

Flowers 'n' Showers Umbrellas

I remember wishing for a parasol when I was a little girl. I loved the romance of this sun-shader and often pretended with my plain umbrella that I was Marlo Thomas. Parasols are difficult to make. So this is my answer to that girl's dream.

I placed the design horizontally on the yellow umbrella and vertically on the pink umbrella. Let your imagination be your guide.

Open the umbrella. Trace a purchased leaf stencil onto fabric or paper. This will make the stencil more pliable to work with. Tape the stencil securely to the umbrella with masking tape.

Hold the open umbrella's handle between your knees. To trace one section at a time, cut a piece of cardboard to fit between the slats of the umbrella structure. Cover the cardboard with a plastic bag and tape it in place. Use a tracing pencil or a marking pen to trace the stencil design. You can use the elements of the stencil in any combination to create an original design. Stencil the entire umbrella. Set the stencil aside and start painting.

Use a brush to fill in the design (you can even use your fingers), working on one panel at a time. If using a sponge on a larger design, squirt some paint onto plastic wrap so you can easily dab the sponge into the paint. Here's a tip: The best sponges for painting are sold in country and western clothing stores and are used to clean Stetsons. They are the perfect size and have the right amount of holes to create a mottled effect with the paint.

Outline the leaves with puff paint. While the paint is still wet, run a toothpick through it to make the veins of the leaves. Wipe the toothpick clean with a paper towel after each use. Fill in each side of each leaf with two different shades of green and then sprinkle clear irides-cent glitter onto the wet paint. Using different colors of puff paint, make dots around each design. As a finishing touch, hot-glue roses, bows, and decorative jewels around the leaves.

Repeat the painting process for each panel of the umbrella, making sure the areas you have worked on previously are dry to prevent smearing.

Let the umbrella dry for at least eight hours.

What to Use

Supplies: Umbrella, fabric paints, puff paints, clear iridescent glitter, ribbon roses, bows, decorative jewels, clear hot-glue sticks, stencil

Tools: White tracing pencil, marking pen, plastic wrap, cardboard, masking tape, paintbrushes, sponge, toothpick, paper towels, hot-glue gun

Keep the umbrella open while you are painting and work on one panel at a time.

Absolutely Amethyst Sweatsuit

Whether running at the gym or just to the store, this two-piece suit will work out for you.

Fold the sweatshirt in half down the front, matching shoulder seams; mark the center with a pin. Then fold the lace insert in half and mark the center with a pin. Match pins and pin insert in place.

Machine-zigzag the insert to the sweatshirt, following the contours of the lace. Turn the shirt inside out.

Trim the shirt fabric from behind the lace, using embroidery scissors. Cut as close as possible to the sewing line so that no excess sweatshirt fleece shows through the lace.

Dye the finished sweatshirt and sweatpants in the same dyebath, following the instructions on pages 122 and 123.

Finish by handstitching a ribbon rose to the sweatshirt.

What to Use

Supplies: White sweatshirt and sweatpants, white lace neckline insert, thread to match, Amethyst #14 powder RIT Dye, ribbon rose

Tools: Straight pins, sewing machine, embroidery scissors, needle

I put a ribbon rose in the middle of the lace to draw further attention to it.

Even Cowgirls Wear the Blues

Turquoise blues, that is. You'll be the sweetheart of the rodeo in your turquoise two-steppers and a custom-painted cowboy shirt to boot.

Boots

Make the large and small rose stencils by tracing the patterns onto the frosted side of plastic template material. Place the plastic onto a protective mat. Cut out the stencils, using a craft knife.

Working on one boot at a time, tape the small rose stencil onto the boot and trace with a pencil. (See photo for more details.) To add more roses, move the stencil around as desired and use different elements of the flower to make your custom version of the design.

Paint the roses and the leaves with turquoise and lavender fabric paints. You'll have better control if you use a brush.

If your boots have stitched designs, paint inside them as desired. Paint clear iridescent glitter paint on the stitched designs on the toes. For a final flourish, dab glitter paint onto the roses, too.

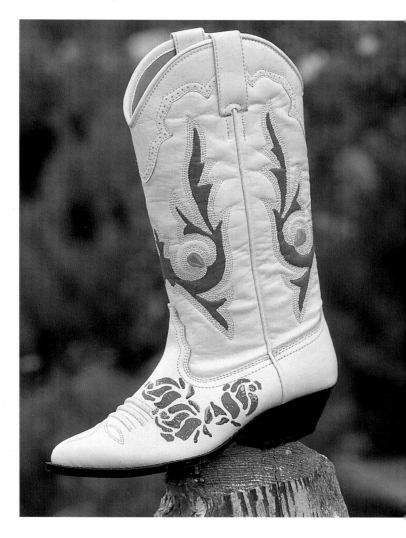

What to Use

Supplies: White cowboy boots, stencil on page 125, plastic template material, protective mat, fabric paint, iridescent glitter paint

Tools: Craft knife, masking tape, pencil, paint, paintbrushes

Shirt

Choose a shirt to decorate. You might have an old shirt you'd like to fix up or practice on. My shirt has white studs on the front placket and the cuffs. If your shirt has regular buttons, you might want to change them to personalize your design.

Select some paints to be applied with paintbrushes and some puff paints that come in squirt bottles for direct application—the variation will give the designs dimension.

Note: Whenever you use puff paint, first try it out on a piece of plastic wrap to make sure the paint flows smoothly from the bottle. A splatter is hard to remove and harder still to decorate around!

Lay the shirt on a table. Place your stencils on an area you want to paint. With a pencil, trace the stencils onto the shirt. Repeat to stencil roses on the collar, the cuffs, the placket, the yoke, and the pockets.

Cover a sheet of shirt cardboard with a plastic bag. Place it under the layer of fabric you are working on to prevent the paint from bleeding through.

Paint the designs. Using a brush, paint the roses turquoise. Apply the paint a little beyond the pencil lines since tracing a stencil makes the design slightly smaller. What's more, the paint covers up the pencil marks. While the paint is still wet, dust clear iridescent glitter onto the rose petals. After the paint dries, add a touch of lavender paint to a few of the tips of the flowers. Then outline some of the petals with silver puff paint, applying it directly from the bottle.

Give the leaves more variety by painting one side of each dark green and the opposite side light green. Add depth with puff paint by using dark green on the dark green side and a lighter green on the other side. Then outline the veins on the light green side with dark green.

Embellish the shirt by hot-gluing turquoise satin bows and ribbon rosebuds to the collar points, the yoke fronts, and the pockets. Randomly hot-glue a few turquoise Austrian crystals to the designs. All of these last-minute inspirations are machine-washable.

What to Use

Supplies: Cowboy shirt in desired color; stencils used for boots; fabric paints in turquoise, lavender, silver, and dark and light green; clear iridescent glitter; turquoise satin bows; turquoise ribbon rosebuds; Austrian crystals; clear hot-glue sticks

Tools: Pencil, plastic wrap, shirt cardboard, plastic bag, paintbrushes, hot-glue gun

The roses on this shirt are painted turquoise, lavender, and silver; light and dark shades of green are used for the leaves.

Bodacious Baby Rompers

These are perfect baby gifts: easy, inexpensive, and absolutely adorable.

Buy a romper one size larger than you want since the hot water needed to set the dye will shrink pure cotton. (On the plus side, it will also make the fabric softer.)

Immerse the romper in a dyebath prepared in the washing machine (see dyeing instructions on pages 122 and 123). When the garment has absorbed enough of the dye to suit your taste, remove and hang to dry. (Use less dye and more water to get a pastel shade.) The garment will dry a slightly lighter color.

Handstitch pastel ribbon roses at the front neckline and at the waist for the yellow romper. Add an aqua bow to the center front and on the left side of the waistline. Cut off three rosettes of sequins in colors to match the ribbon roses and sew them down the center front to simulate buttons. (Sequin rosettes come in long strings, attached to individual net backing.)

Handstitch a lace ruffle around the neckline and down the front for the pink romper. Add four ribbon roses over the ruffle. For an accent, stitch a scrap of lace and a ribbon rose at the hip.

Always use nontoxic materials when working with baby clothes and make sure garments are flame retardant.

Note: Stitch all embellishments carefully. They could be harmful if swallowed by a baby. Use soft and baby-safe decorations.

What to Use

Supplies: Plain white 100%-cotton baby romper, liquid RIT Dye in desired color, ribbon roses, sequin roses, lace ruffle, thread to match

Tools: Washing machine, needle, scissors

Crystal Bustier and Tuxedo Jacket

I love to wear this outfit because it is utterly feminine, especially the bustier. Here, I wear it with the pink-washed tuxedo jacket. I also like to put it under a plain tailored blazer or a blue jeans jacket.

Bustier

Buy the best ecru long-line strapless bra you can afford. Shop for it in the lingerie section of a department or specialty store. You might even find what you like at a lingerie party. While a good bra is expensive, quality really makes a difference for this project.

Start by putting on your bra (from here on, we'll refer to it as a bustier). If it's more convenient, slip it on a dress form that duplicates your figure. Either way, stretching the bustier is essential to make sure the embellishments are placed properly.

Pin the lace motifs to the bustier. Use a large white bridal lace appliqué in a long V shape for the main motif. Pin the lace on while wearing the bustier and then remove it to handstitch the appliqué in place. Because this bustier had a lovely lace front to begin with, it only needed a little more lace.

Clip scraps of cream passementerie lace into swirling shapes and stitch them along the bustline. (You don't have to put the bustier back on for this because you are working on a part of the garment that doesn't need to be stretched.)

To finish, place a small beaded appliqué (from the bridal department) front and center. Glue a porcelain rose button on top of the appliqué. Randomly hot-glue pastel-colored and clear Austrian crystals and flat-backed pearls all over the appliqués.

What to Use

Supplies: Ecru long-line strapless bra, large and small bridal lace appliqués, scraps of cream passementerie lace, porcelain rose button, pastel-colored and clear Austrian crystals, flat-backed pearls, clear hot-glue sticks, thread to match

Tools: Dress form (optional), straight pins, scissors, needle, hot-glue gun

Jacket

Shop for a white tuxedo jacket at a formal-wear rental shop. Jackets retired from stock are often available for sale. Or browse through a thrift or consignment shop.

Machine-wash the jacket before you begin. This is a white polyester boy's jacket with a nylon lining. (The nylon dyes a slightly different color than the body of the jacket. You can capitalize on this difference when you roll up the sleeves.)

Mix a combination of Ecru, Rose Pink, and a few drops of Cocoa Brown RIT Dye in the washing machine. See pages 122 and 123 for dyeing instructions. When the dye is the desired shade, quickly dip the white beaded appliqués into the dyebath to give them a tint of color. Remove them and set aside to dry. Then immerse the jacket until the desired color is achieved.

Dry the jacket in the dryer, throwing in a fabric softener sheet to make the jacket easier to work with.

Spread the embellishments over the lapels. Completely cover the lapels with white, pale pink, and deep rose passementerie lace; pink-and-white striped satin ribbon; pink ribbon roses; and the tinted appliqués. Hot-glue the larger pieces first and then fill in with Austrian crystals. Cut some of the beaded appliqués to fit at the bottom of the lapels. Embellish the pocket as desired to carry the color and the sparkle onto the jacket.

To customize your design, replace the buttons with porcelain rose buttons. This jacket had two buttons and no buttonhole, so the buttons were replaced with porcelain rose buttons. Two more of the rose buttons balance each other a bit farther up on the jacket front, right on the darts. Hot-glue a pin back to a fifth button on the upper left lapel, and you have a brooch.

What to Use

Supplies: White tuxedo jacket; Ecru #18, Rose Pink #7, and Cocoa Brown #20 RIT Dye; beaded lace appliqués; scraps of white, pale pink, and deep rose passementerie lace; pink-and-white striped satin ribbon; pink ribbon roses; Austrian crystals; pink porcelain rose buttons; pin back; thread to match; clear hot-glue sticks

Tools: Washing machine, hot-glue gun, needle, scissors

The secret to success with this project is to not worry too much about symmetry. Just please yourself. Thanks to the pocket, there are more embellishments on the left side of my jacket than on the right—and I like it like that!

Rosy Robe

I found this plain white robe minus its sash for a pittance at a discount store. A quick dye job and a rose-printed cotton were all I needed to jazz it up!

Dye the robe, following the directions on pages 122 and 123.

Trace the pockets onto tissue paper, adding ⅜" seam allowances. Cut them out from the fabric and press under the seam allowances on all pieces. Pin them in place. Use either a straight stitch or a narrow zigzag to sew the appliqués onto the pockets.

Cut out shapes for the lapel appliqués, using the fabric design as your guide. If you are cutting out a motif from a printed fabric, outline the motif with liquid ravel preventer first and let it dry. Then cut around the edges of the treated area. This will give you a clean-edged appliqué. Place the appliqués where desired on the collar and the pockets and stitch them to the robe, using a narrow zigzag.

Replace the belt, if desired, with a length of satin drapery cording with tassels for a more elegant look. Although nothing was done to the cuffs, don't let that stop you!

What to Use

Supplies: White terry cloth robe, Peach #48 RIT Dye, floral print fabric, thread to match, rayon satin drapery cording with tassels (optional)

Tools: Washing machine, tissue paper, scissors, straight pins, liquid ravel preventer, sewing machine

For the belt, I thought satin drapery cording with tassels was a fun addition. If the robe had had a belt, I might have sewn more fabric appliqués to it. Follow your instincts when embellishing your robe.

Sunflower Jeans Jacket

This design shows how I can't leave well enough alone. With all the flowers and the lace I added, this jacket is just as pretty half a mile away as it is close up!

Cut two panels of white passementerie lace for the front of the jacket, cutting each panel to a point on the lower edge. This will disguise the front welt pockets but still allow them to be functional. Hot-glue the lace in place.

Hot-glue sunflowers along the shoulder seams. This theme is echoed by stitching sunflower buttons to the front lace panels.

Glue daisy chain lace along the gussets of the jacket front. Cut an individual daisy from the same trim for each stud. Cut into each and take out a small part of the center. Then hot-glue one beneath each stud on the jacket front and on the cuffs so that the brown stud forms the center.

Hot-glue lengths of white fringed lace along the shoulder seams. Hot-glue small sunflowers along the shoulder seam fringe. Two more sunflowers accent the top of each front side pocket.

What to Use

Supplies: Blue denim jacket, passementerie lace, poly-silk sunflowers, sunflower buttons, clear hot-glue sticks, daisy chain lace, white fringed lace, small poly-silk golden sunflowers, thread to match,

Tools: Scissors, hot-glue gun, needle

When I first started making clothes, my brother, Freddy, described my style as Levi Strauss meets Liberace.

Pearls & Lace Cotton Sweater

I bought this sweater with the pretty white pearl buttons already in place, so all I had to do was add a bit of lace to dress it up.

Edge a few large flowers in the lace with liquid ravel preventer. When dry, cut each out, trimming close to the line of ravel preventer.

Pin the lace cutouts to the sweater front as desired. When you are pleased with the arrangement, machine-stitch them with a narrow zigzag. Hot-glue flat-backed pearls here and there in between the roses.

Handstitch a rose motif from the lace on top of the Battenberg lace appliqué. On the unadorned side of the sweater front, machine-stitch the appliqué along the side and bottom edges to make a pocket.

Border the neckline and the front edge of the sweater with white picot trim. Machine-stitch down the middle of the trim, using a narrow zigzag.

What to Use

Supplies: Black button-front sweater, white lace with floral motif, liquid ravel preventer, flat-backed pearls, large Battenberg lace appliqué, white picot trim, thread to match, clear hot-glue sticks

Tools: Sewing machine, straight pins, needle, scissors, hot-glue gun

This plain black sweater was transformed in a matter of minutes with a little bit of lace and pearls.

I-Could-Have-Danced-All-Night
Evening Bag and Pumps

Fashion a purse and a pair of pumps to cap off an evening stunner. Being able to color-coordinate accessories with your eveningwear will give you so much flexibility.

Purchase satin high-heeled pumps and a matching evening bag. Some stores that sell these items will dye them for you, but it can take as long as two weeks to get them back. If you've been invited to a soirée on short notice, dye the pumps and the bag yourself.

Select some beaded lace appliqués to dress up your dyeable basics. You can use small scraps left over from other projects.

Dye all the items, including the appliqués and the lace, in a dyebath of Aquamarine, Mint Green, and Teal, referring to the instructions on pages 122 and 123. Attach a string to the inside of the purse lining, using a safety pin. Wearing rubber gloves, place the shoes and

Do not put embellishments on the inner sides of your shoes—you will dance them right off!

the purse into the dyebath and swish them around with a wooden spoon. (If you dye these pieces in the washing machine, don't let the agitator run.) The trick is to get all items to spend the same amount of time in the dyebath so that they all turn out the same shade. Be careful not to hold on to the items as you place them in the dyebath. The dye will not take as strongly where your fingers grasp the fabric, and you'll end up with blotchy dyeables. When removing or checking for color, lift the shoes by the very tips of the heels or with a wooden spoon. Raise the purse by grasping the string.

Let the items dry. Set the shoes upright and hang the purse by the string.

To decorate the purse, hot-glue the beaded lace appliqués to the front flap. Hot-glue lace trim around the flap. Add a few Austrian crystals and flat-backed pearls, along with several ribbon rosebuds. To decorate the shoes, hot-glue lace trim around the shoes and glue appliqués on the front and the outer sides. Add ribbon roses and flat-backed pearls to the appliqués. Finally, to make you look even lighter on your feet, hot-glue a few Austrian crystals to the appliqués and at regular intervals on the ribbon around the shoes.

What to Use

Supplies: White satin evening bag; white satin pumps; Aquamarine #24, Mint Green #8, and Teal #4 RIT Dye; beaded lace appliqués; narrow lace trim; Austrian crystals; flat-backed pearls; ribbon rosebuds; clear hot-glue sticks

Tools: Washing machine (optional), rubber gloves, wooden spoon, hot-glue gun

Dress Redress

Sometimes the only thing you end up saving from your wedding day is your wedding dress. I know that was the case with my first wedding dress. This is the gown I designed and wore at my first wedding (see the photo above). I think it was the highlight of the event. Many women save their wedding dresses but never wear them again. The same thing happens to bridesmaids' dresses. Why not revamp a cherished or not-so-cherished dress and make it work for another occasion?

My dress redo was quite involved. Because of that the how-tos really don't belong in this book. But the idea certainly does, and I hope that the transformation inspires you to try a similar change on a gown of your own.

Summer

I remember ice-cream clouds, sun-kissed noses, and adventure-filled days with my grandfather in a little town where time stood still.

No matter what the excitement of the day, our evenings would always end with a trip to get ice cream. Grampy would hold me up to the window, and I'd say, "I'd like a soft chocolate swirl dipped in peppermint with sprinkles, please." And Grampy would add, "Make mine vanilla." As summers went by, I realized "make mine vanilla" was my grandfather's reaction to anything new-fangled or new-fashioned. He liked things simple. So whether it's dipped in sparkles or sprinkled with pearls, I'm thinking of Grampy as I tell you, "Just *don't* make mine vanilla."

Meadow Flowers Sun Hat

My buddy Spencer and I know the essential element for any ladylike picnic: a bonnet!

I used green velvet ribbon for my hat because it reminded me of a paper hat my mom made for me for a parade at school.

Purchase a plain hat that suits you. If you must buy one that is adorned, remove the trim and save it for a future project.

If you want to reshape the hat, turning the brim up or down, it's easy to do. Spritz the brim with water until damp and then place the hat on your head. While looking in the mirror, hold the brim in place with one hand and use a blow dryer with the other. Respritz as needed to get the desired shape.

Cover the crown of the hat with a circle of pink lace fabric left over from In-the-Pink Fringed Shawl project (on page 12). Hot-glue the fabric in place around the base of the crown.

I hot-glued pink braid to the edges of forest green ribbon and wrapped the ribbon around the crown.

Embellish the hat with ribbon. Before gluing the ribbon band in place, make a corsage bow (see the bow instructions on page 112). Try on the hat in front of a mirror and move the bow around until you find where it looks best. Then glue the ribbon band in place and cover the cut ends with the bow.

Hot-glue poly-silk flowers to the bow. This hat has antiqued silk roses in a variety of colors, emerald sequined leaves, turquoise foil leaves, and silk leaves. Red-and-white silk butterflies landed on it and wouldn't leave!

What to Use

Supplies: Plain straw hat, pink lace fabric, clear hot-glue sticks, green velvet ribbon, pink braid, poly-silk flowers, sequined leaves, foil leaves, silk leaves, silk butterflies

Tools: Spray bottle filled with water, blow dryer, scissors, hot-glue gun

Peach Lacy Sweater

Clothes that can be dressed up or down are so versatile. This sweater looks great with shorts for play or with a suit for work.

Center and pin the bridal appliqué on the front of the cotton sweater. Handstitch it in place. Either handstitch or hot-glue ribbon rosebuds to the lace as desired. Hot-glue pearl clusters to the sweater (see the photo). This is an easy project that will be ready to wear in minutes.

What to Use

Supplies: Plain peach cotton sleeveless sweater, large V-shaped bridal lace appliqué, thread to match, peach ribbon rosebuds, pearl clusters, clear hot-glue sticks

Tools: Straight pins, needle, thimble, hot-glue gun

Sometimes a beautiful bridal appliqué is sold already beaded. If your appliqué or lace is bare, simply hot-glue or stitch some pearls or beads on the appliqué.

Jazzy June Jeans

When I was in junior high school, I used to save my money to buy special jeans at a favorite store in Hollywood. I loved jeans that were studded and trimmed with lace. I never got over that phase, so here is my version, making old jeans look cute again.

Place tissue paper on the back pocket of your jeans. Trace with a tracing pencil or pen to make a pattern. Repeat on the front side of the jeans, tracing the inside of the left pocket and the small pocket inside the large pocket on the right. Cut out the patterns from the pink lace fabric, adding ⅜" seam allowances.

Turn the seam allowances under and pin them in place. Press with a damp pressing cloth to steam the lace pieces without damaging the fabric. Apply the various lace pieces to the corresponding pockets. Topstitch them in place, using a straight stitch or a very narrow zigzag. Handstitch the lace in place at the top of the pockets.

Measure and cut lengths of pink floral trim to accent the top of the pockets, the side seam of each leg, and the sides of the back pockets. To make sure pockets remain functional, hot-glue or handstitch the trim in place.

What to Use

Supplies: Denim jeans (new or old), pink lace fabric, thread to match, pink floral trim, clear hot-glue sticks

Tools: Tissue paper, tracing pencil or pen, scissors, straight pins, sewing machine, hot-glue gun

For these pink floral trimmed jeans, I selected a brand that has distinctive pockets for adding lace. Whichever brand you choose, use your own judgment in placing the lace.

Princess Pretties

Little girls, including Spencer, have fun dressing up like fairy princesses. Since it's not always appropriate to wear a tiara on the playground, I'll show you how to make fancy headbands and hair bows that are fit for royalty but made especially for your favorite girl.

Ribbons & Roses Headband

Put a tiny dab of hot glue on the underside of the headband at one end. Press one end of the ribbon into the glue to hold it firmly in place. Let it dry. Wrap the ribbon to completely cover the headband, pulling the ribbon tightly as you work. Occasionally add a dab of glue to make sure the ribbon doesn't slip out of place. Trim the excess ribbon and hot-glue the free end to the underside of the band.

Use the same or contrasting ribbon to make a bow. A double-looped bow will give the finished headband a headdress look. Wire the bow loops together at the center with florist's wire. Try the headband on the girl to determine the right spot, taking in consideration her facial structure and hairstyle. When you are satisfied with the look, remove the headband and hot-glue the bow in place.

Cut two lengths of rosebud ribbon. Hot-glue in place under the bow so that the ribbons cascade down the side of the headband. There are many other ways to add a finishing touch. Your fairy princess probably has some ideas of her own.

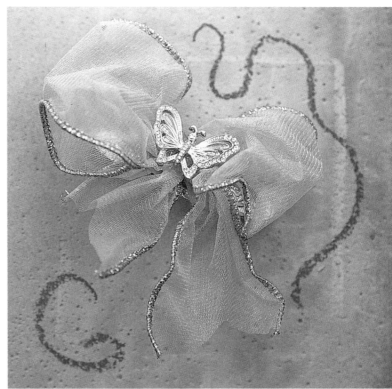

Pretty-in-Pink Hair Ornament

Tie a bow with pink satin wire-edged French ribbon and hot-glue it to a plain hair clip. Fold over a small scrap of ribbon left over from the headband project and glue it to the center of the bow. Then hot-glue the silk flowers in place. Since little girls love pink, choose flowers in two shades of the color.

Blue Angel Bow Clip

Make a simple bow and hot-glue it to a hair clip. Nestle a butterfly button (left over from the Flutterby Butterfly Blouse on page 66) in the center of the bow and hot-glue it in place. The airy delicacy of this ribbon will make you think of fairies or angels.

What to Use

Supplies: Clear hot-glue sticks, plain plastic headband, assorted craft ribbons (wire-edged and plain), florist's wire, satin rosebud ribbon, plain hair clips, silk flowers, gold butterfly button

Tools: Scissors, hot-glue gun

Sunbathing Beauty Cover-up

I have always been fascinated by the glamour and the clothes of the movie stars in the thirties and the forties. The fashions of that period never fail to inspire me. That's why I designed this lacy cover-up. It reminds me of something Ginger Rogers might have worn.

Lay the tablecloth flat on the floor. Fold it in half. Measure and mark the center point along the folded edge. Mark the neckline with pins. Cut out a circle for the neckline and then cut the opening for the front. (Many tablecloths have a small center design; that was used here for the neckline opening.)

Treat the cut edges with liquid ravel preventer and let dry. Fold the hem under ⅜". Pin the braid along the hem, turning the cut ends of the braid under for a clean finish. Machine-stitch down the middle of the braid with either a straight stitch or a narrow zigzag, depending on the type of braid.

Place the ribbon lace trim ½" away from the braid and machine-stitch it in place.

Fold the tablecloth in half, with the front opening at the center. Measure and mark 18" from the fold on each side. Tack the front and back sides together at the marks to create sleeves.

To finish each shoulder area, starting at the sleeve edge and ending approximately 2" from the neck edge, weave two strands of ecru satin ribbon in and out of the lace. Pull the ribbons on each end to gather the fabric. Tie a bow at each end to secure the ribbons. Tack the bows in place.

What to Use

Supplies: White or ecru 72"-diameter rayon-cotton blend round lace tablecloth (new or old), cream rayon braid, ribbon lace trim, narrow cream satin ribbon, thread to match

Tools: Scissors, liquid ravel preventer, straight pins, sewing machine, needle, ruler, thimble

I used an unusual ruffled ribbon design on a netting background for the trim.

Swanky Shades

If you can't be a movie star, just look like one. I wear my sunglasses about 90% of the time, day and night. To me, they are part and parcel of movie star status. The pair I'm wearing looks like a million dollar deal.

To begin, look through your trinkets and choose your favorite items. Think about where you'll put them on your sunglasses. You can make a sketch of where you want to place the embellishments or just picture the design in your mind's eye and start gluing!

Be sure to use enough glue to hold the decorations in place but not so much that the glue shows. Hot glue is more noticeable against black than any other color, but you can wipe off excess glue with a cotton swab. Use a toothpick, if necessary, to move pieces around.

To make the black sunglasses (top left), use black Austrian crystals and heart-shaped faux

When I was young I wasn't into Elton John's music, but I *was* into his glasses. I thought they were really cool.

enamel buttons. Once you have decided on placement, hot-glue them in place.

Hot-glue pearls to brown tortoiseshell sunglasses (middle left) for a more sophisticated look.

Hot-glue hot pink crystals and pale pink porcelain roses to iridescent brown-and-gold sunglasses (bottom left). Add small gold cherubs in the center of each design.

Let each project dry completely. Be sure to keep the sunglasses in a case when you are not wearing them.

What to Use

Supplies: Sunglasses, Austrian crystals in assorted colors, decorative buttons, pearls, gold jewelry parts, porcelain roses, clear hot-glue sticks

Tools: Hot-glue gun, cotton swabs, toothpicks (optional)

Footloose and Fancy-free

Who wants to wear seriously stuffy shoes in the summer? Not me! So I made floral flip-flops by covering them with ribbons and roses. And my linen boots are a hoot when they bloom with hand-painted flowers.

Froufrou Flip-flops

Dab a bead of hot glue on the underside of the strap at the botton of one side. Wrap the ribbon until one side is completely covered. Anchor the ribbon at the bottom of the toe piece with hot glue. Continue wrapping to the end of the other side of the strap. Trim the excess ribbon and secure the cut end with another dab of glue.

If you run out of ribbon before covering both sides of the strap, join pieces with a dot of glue on the underside of the strap and continue wrapping. Using your fingers, press all glue dots flat when partially set. Remember, your feet will be sensitive to any lumps on the underside of the straps.

Hot-glue a silk flower onto the strap of each flip-flop.

What to Use

Supplies: Flip-flops, clear hot-glue sticks, plain or floral ribbon, silk flowers

Tools: Hot-glue gun, scissors

Hot-glue a silk flower onto the strap once it is covered.

I painted delicate forget-me-nots freehand on the shoes, using fabric paint.

Forget-me-not Linen Hightops

Make sure the shoes are thoroughly clean before applying paint, especially if you are disguising hand-me-downs.

Practice painting on a paper towel if you're not comfortable with your artistic ability.

Sketch your design and then paint the boots as desired.

What to Use

Supplies: White canvas or linen hightops (or shoes of your choice), fabric paint in assorted colors, paper towels (optional)

Tool: Paintbrushes

Rhinestone Love

I think that rhinestones-by-the-yard look a lot like tennis bracelets. So why not wrap rhinestones all over your tennis togs?

Even though this project is understated, you can create a more elaborate version. Dye the shirt first in your signature color, add sew-on jewels to the collar and the cuffs, or stitch on an appliqué.

Smashing Tennis Shirt

Handstitch the rhinestone trim to the edge of the shirt collar, carefully securing the first and last rhinestones to prevent them from falling off when the string joining them is cut. (Liquid ravel preventer can also help to avoid this problem.) Repeat to add trim along the edge of the front placket.

Replace the original buttons with buttons of your choice.

Enlarge the buttonholes, if necessary, by using a single-edged razor blade. Whipstitch the newly cut area of each buttonhole or secure the raw edges with liquid ravel preventer.

What to Use

Supplies: Plain white ladies' golf shirt, rhinestones-by-the-yard trim, fancy buttons, thread to match

Tools: Needle, single-edged razor blade, liquid ravel preventer

Light-on-Your-Feet Lace Sneakers

Hot-glue rhinestone trim around the edge of each shoe where the fabric meets the white rubber sole. Then hot-glue a strip of rhinestones across the cap of the toe (see the photo for details).

Cut individual flowers from daisy chain lace trim and hot-glue them to the front of each toe.

In the center of each daisy, hot-glue a pastel-colored Austrian crystal. It's as simple as that!

What to Use

Supplies: White lace tennis shoes, rhinestones-by-the-yard trim, daisy chain lace trim, Austrian crystals in assorted pastel colors, clear hot-glue sticks

Tools: Scissors, hot-glue gun

Camellia-Kissed Visor

Wrap a narrow strip of lace on the band of an inexpensive visor and cut the lace to fit. Treat the cut ends of the lace with liquid ravel preventer. Glue the lace in place.

Hot-glue the camellia to the brim as far to one side as it will go without extending over the edges. Hot-glue clear Austrian crystals to the tight swirls of the lace.

What to Use

Supplies: White cloth-covered visor, narrow lace embellishment, silk camellia, clear Austrian crystals, clear hot-glue sticks

Tools: Scissors, liquid ravel preventer, hot-glue gun

Summer Belt Buckle

This project gives you a chance to use what you have on hand or items you have found on shopping expeditions. When it comes to decorating and embellishing, remember that my motto is Less Is Never More.

Jewelry parts and Austrian crystals are all you need to add a little personality to your favorite belt.

Wipe the metal buckle with acetone or nail polish remover to take off any finish. This will improve the bond with the glue.

Glue the desired items in place with jewelry cement or hot glue (this dries faster) until the entire buckle is covered. Position the biggest pieces first. Let the glue set before adding the smaller items on top.

To finish, fill in any gaps with hot glue. Press Austrian crystals or charms into the wet glue. Let the buckle sit undisturbed overnight to dry, making sure the jewelry parts don't shift.

I pulled this belt out of my closet and transformed it with flowers. You could do the same with an old belt or an inexpensive new one.

If you need to reposition something, heat the glue again with a blow dryer.

What to Use

Supplies: Simple belt with plain wide metal buckle, jewelry cement (optional), clear hot-glue sticks, flower jewelry parts, gold metal charms, assorted decorative buttons, Austrian crystals

Tools: Acetone or nail polish remover, hot-glue gun

There's No Place Like Oz

I love *The Wizard of Oz!* As a little girl I wanted ruby slippers. As a big girl I wanted ruby slippers. So I finally surrendered to my inner Dorothy and followed my heart right down the yellow brick road.

Ruby Slippers

Make sure recycled shoes are clean by using a commercial shoe cleaner. Fluff up some tissue paper or paper towels and wrap them around one hand. Place the wrapped hand inside a plastic bag. Working on one shoe at a time, place this hand inside a shoe. This will protect your hand and the inside of the shoes from the shoe cleaner.

To dye the shoes, follow the instructions on pages 40 and 41 and let them dry half a day. If you are using leather shoes, you must first score the leather, following the instructions on pages 90 and 91.

Make two bows out of grosgrain ribbon or out of sequin trim. Pinch each in the middle and secure with wire. Hot-glue a small piece of ribbon on top of each piece of wire to cover. If using grosgrain ribbon, hot-glue crystals or sequins to the ribbon pieces to make them sparkle.

Put the bows on the top of the shoes and mark placement of each with a pen. Hot-glue Austrian crystals in a pattern around the front and the outer sides. Paint the shoes, except the heels, with a coat of Aleene's Tacky Glue. (You can use other glues, but this one allows the glitter to adhere the best.) You can even put glue on the sides of the Austrian crystals. While the glue is wet, sprinkle glitter on the shoes until they are thoroughly covered.

Hot-glue sequin trim around the edge of each shoe for a finished look. Hot-glue the bows in place.

What to Use

Supplies: Red shoes (or light-colored shoes and Scarlet #5 RIT Dye), 1½" - to 2"-wide red grosgrain ribbon or sequin trim, red Austrian crystals, clear hot-glue sticks, Aleene's Tacky Glue, red glitter, ¼"-wide red sequin trim

Tools: Tissue paper or paper towels, plastic bag, scissors, hot-glue gun, tweezers (optional)

Pet Collars

Buy a collar and take it with you to select the right color and width of braid. Choose loosely woven braid because it allows the catch to easily fit through the holes. Cut the braid equal to the length of the collar and hot-glue the ends in place. Use Tacky Glue to keep the length of braid in place. Use liquid ravel preventer or a little hot glue to keep the ends from fraying. Hot-glue flowers or other embellishments to the collar.

What to Use

Supplies: Nylon dog collar, loosely woven decorative braid, silk flowers or other embellishments, clear hot-glue sticks, Aleene's Tacky Glue

Tools: Hot-glue gun, scissors

This collar is best for young dogs who are used to wearing something around their necks. Remember to add an identification tag for security.

Flutterby Butterfly Blouse

Discount stores are great places to find inexpensive basics like this blouse. But when you're through adding embellishments, your blouse will look neither basic nor inexpensive!

Remove the original buttons and dye the blouse in the washing machine. See pages 122 and 123 for dyeing instructions.

Make a pattern for the lace collar and cuffs. Spread the blouse flat on your work surface. Lay some tissue paper on the areas to be covered with lace. Trace the patterns, adding ⅜" seam allowances. (Any less does not allow room for error and any more is too much.)

Fold the lace fabric in half. Fold the collar pattern in half. Match the folds and pin the pattern in place. Cut out a single pattern piece. Turn up the ⅜" seam allowance and press.

Pin the lace to the collar, aligning outside edges. Straightstitch the pieces together as close to the edge of the collar as possible. You can trim some of the excess seam allowance first if you think it will show through the finished collar. If you cut too close, use liquid ravel preventer to keep the lace from fraying. Tuck the inner edge of the lace collar into the neckline of the blouse and handstitch it in place.

Align one edge of the cuff pattern with the fold of the lace. Cut out one lace piece for each cuff. Pin and stitch in place, following the directions for the collar.

Hot-glue the butterfly appliqués to the right side of the blouse. (I'm a fan of shortcuts so I used glue, but you might prefer to stitch the appliqués on instead.) Hot-glue Austrian crystals to the wings. Replace the original buttons with butterfly buttons.

What to Use

Supplies: Plain white blouse, Ecru #18 and Rose Pink #7 RIT Dye, approximately ½ yard of 36"-wide white-and-gold lace fabric, two butterfly appliqués, topaz and clear Austrian crystals, butterfly buttons, clear hot-glue sticks, thread to match

Tools: Washing machine, tissue paper, scissors, sewing machine, hot-glue gun, tracing pen or pencil, straight pins, needle, thimble

I adore butterflies so much that I surround myself with them at home—framed above the mantel, painted on the walls, and hung as magnets on my refrigerator!

Fishing for Compliments

Like a lot of girls, Spencer loves to dress up and kid around. We're remaining cool while wearing our jeweled denim jackets as we haul in a keeper—Spencer's embellished tennis shoe!

A little dye and some daisy chain lace turn these ordinary sneakers into something pretty special.

Hightop Tennis Shoes

Remember to buy the shoes a little bigger, as dyeing may shrink them a size.

To dye the tennis shoes, wet them thoroughly and then gently place them into a well-mixed dyebath in the washing machine. Let the shoes air-dry thoroughly. See pages 122 and 123 for dyeing instructions.

Hot-glue the daisy chain lace around the edge of each shoe where the fabric meets the sole. Alternate gluing a rosebud and an Austrian crystal in the center of the daisies. Add an

My jacket's white on white so I can wear it on chilly summer evenings at home in Malibu. Spencer's jacket is decorated with colored jewels and is made similarly to mine.

aqua satin bow on each toe and hot-glue an Austrian crystal in the center of each bow.

What to Use

Supplies: White high-heeled kids' canvas shoes, Aquamarine #24 RIT Dye, daisy chain lace, pale aqua rosebuds, turquoise Austrian crystals, two aqua satin bows, clear hot-glue sticks

Tools: Scissors, hot-glue gun

The collar was graced with pieces of lace and floral sequin-and-bead motifs.

Jeweled Denim Jacket

Big or little, a denim jacket is a real wardrobe workhorse, looking great at a glitzy resort or at a backyard barbeque.

Lay out all the embellishments as desired on the jacket before attaching them. Place two large V-shaped bridal lace appliqués under the pocket flaps for the front panels and hot-glue them in place. Make a collage of lace scraps and beaded and sequined appliqués on the upper parts of the jacket. The collar gets a symmetrical treatment with a piece of lace and a floral sequin-and-bead motif on each side. Hot-glue them in place.

Hot-glue clear Austrian crystals randomly over the embellished areas.

If you want the two front pockets to remain functional, be careful to leave the flaps free. Plain studs are dark and utilitarian, so hot-glue a few Austrian crystals to each. This results in expensive-looking rhinestone studs. Hot-glue an iridescent sequined leaf underneath each stud for a sparkling touch.

For Spencer's blue denim jacket, choose brightly colored appliqués or scraps. Decide on placement and then hot-glue them in place. Hot-glue ribbon rosebuds to the studs.

What to Use

Supplies: White denim jacket (new or old), lace appliqués, lace scraps, clear Austrian crystals, beaded and sequined embellishments, clear hot-glue sticks

Tools: Hot-glue gun, scissors, straight pins

Fall

reminds me of a recurring dream....

I'm stepping up to the podium to claim my Oscar when Dad's voice wakes me. "Today's the first day of school," he says, uttering the phrase that turns a star-studded dream into a nightmare. "But why do I have to go?" I ask. "So you can go into business," Dad says, picking up his briefcase. "So you can be a fashion designer," Mom says, straightening my sweater. "But I'm going to be an actress," I correct them, as they gently shove me out the door....

My most important lesson was not from school but from something my parents somehow knew. The value of my education was learning when to take my cue.

Victorian Vest

I love the look of frilly laces on a man's waistcoat. The turnabout is absolutely charming.

Find a vest that fits you (try a thrift shop) or "borrow" the vest from one of your husband's old three-piece suits. Remove the buttons and keep them for another project.

Put the vest on a flat surface. Cut and piece white lace scraps as desired. Enhance the neckline of the vest with the lace scraps as desired.

Place similar lace scraps on the pocket flaps. Then arrange a few leftover pieces along the lower edges of the vest. Once you are pleased with the overall design, pin the lace pieces in place so they won't move while you are working. Then hot-glue or handstitch them in place.

Stitch new buttons to the vest (cameo buttons were used here). Randomly attach a few Victorian charms and crocheted flowers with pearl centers to the lace pieces. Then hot-glue Austrian crystals on the lace as desired.

What to Use

Supplies: Man's vest, white lace scraps, decorative buttons, Victorian charms, small beige crocheted flowers with pearl centers, Austrian crystals, thread to match, clear hot-glue sticks

Tools: Scissors, straight pins, hot-glue gun, needle

I practically live in vests during the fall, and this one can go from casual to dressy in no time.

Cabbage Roses Vest

For an anniversary present, my father bought my mother something she had always wanted: a flower shop. Its influence on me was profound. While designing wedding bouquets, I realized that flowers and lace were made for each other.

Find a man's vest at a thrift store or steal an old one from your husband's closet. Fashion lapels by handstitching a length of gathered cream lace on each side of the vest (see the photo), folding the cut ends to the inside of the vest at the beginning and the end. Repeat with lengths of pink lace, placing each length approximately 1" from the bound edge of the cream lace. Using Aleene's OK to Wash-It Glue, add silk cabbage roses along the neckline, covering the bottom edge of the pink lace lengths. Glue satin rosebuds to the lace around the roses. Make two bows from pearls-by-the-yard trim. Referring to the photo, hot-glue one bow among the roses on each side of the vest.

Grasp one doily in the center and tuck it into a vest pocket to simulate a hankie. Handstitch it in place. Repeat with the remaining doily and pocket. Glue a silk rose to one side of each pocket. To finish, tie pearls-by-the-yard trim into two bows and glue one under each rose (see the photo).

Hot-glue satin roses to the buttons. Enlarge the buttonholes if needed, using a single-edged razor blade. Seal the cut edges with liquid ravel preventer.

What to Use

Supplies: Man's vest, cream and pink gathered lace, silk cabbage roses in assorted colors, cream satin rosebuds, pearls-by-the-yard trim, cream crocheted doilies, Aleene's OK to Wash-It Glue, clear hot-glue sticks, thread to match, liquid ravel preventer (optional)

Tools: Needle, hot-glue gun, single-edged razor blade (optional)

Bows tied from pearls-by-the-yard trim add a finishing touch to the bouquet of roses on this vest.

Cranberry Chapeau

Fedoras have a tailored look. The felt has a rich texture that can be paired with any outfit. Although I crowned my hat with floral frills, you might wrap yours in burlap and rope.

To decorate a basic felt hat, wrap ivory brocade ribbon around the crown. Trim any excess. Make a bow from the remaining ribbon. Try on the hat in front of a mirror and move the bow around until you find where it looks best. Then glue the ribbon band in place and cover the cut ends with the bow.

Embellish by hot-gluing green silk leaves and silk ribbon roses to the bow. Then hot-glue on pieces of gold ribbon and lace and add some gold sprigs.

What to Use

Supplies: Felt hat, wide ivory wire-edged brocade ribbon, green silk leaves, silk ribbon roses, gold ribbon, gold reembroidered lace, gold bead florist's sprigs, clear hot-glue sticks

Tools: Embroidery scissors, hot-glue gun

I enjoy wearing hats any time of the year, but a hat isn't my hat until I have given it my touch.

Cover Girl Cardigans

There once was a simple sweater I wore to death. Its shape was perfect, but its color was faded and pale. Not only did it become my first dye experiment but also my first embellished sweater. Now no plain sweater is safe with me!

Ribbons and Roses Sweater

Remove the buttons from the sweater unless you want them to pick up color from the dye. (A number of buttons available will dye, others won't, and some will take the color strangely.) Or you may want to replace the buttons with decorative ones that will better suit the sweater's new look.

Select ribbon roses (olive green, mint green, deep peach, and taupe were used here). Using Scarlet, Rose Pink, Peach, and Cocoa Brown, mix a dye-bath that works well with the colors of the roses (see pages 122 and 123 for the dyeing instructions). Dip a paper towel or a washcloth into the dyebath to check the color. Then place the sweater into the washer. When you are satisfied with the color, lay the sweater flat to dry.

When mixing a dyebath of many different colors, use a small amount of each to get a unique shade like this.

Handstitch ribbon roses along the neckline. Roll up the sleeves once and stitch roses in place on the turned-back cuffs.

Replace the buttons with decorative ones. Enlarge the buttonholes if needed, using a single-edged razor blade. Seal the cut edges with liquid ravel preventer.

What to Use

Supplies: White or ivory cardigan sweater; Scarlet #5, Rose Pink #7, Peach #48, and Cocoa Brown #20 RIT Dye; satin ribbon roses in fall tones; decorative buttons (optional); thread to match; liquid ravel preventer (optional)

Tools: Washing machine, needle, single-edged razor blade (optional)

These cameo buttons dress up the sweater and match the new sweater color exactly.

Pointelle Perfection

Remove the original buttons if you don't want them to pick up the dye or if you want to replace them with decorative buttons.

Dye a knit sweater in a mixture of Ecru and Tan, following the directions for dyeing on pages 122 and 123.

Pin variegated reembroidered lace at the neckline (olive green, ecru, and slate blue were used here). Handstitch the lace in place.

Add faux pockets to the lower front. Tint two pieces of Battenberg lace by dipping them quickly in and out of the dyebath. Let them dry. Fold them over to form flaps and hand-stitch them in place to simulate pockets (see the photo for placement). As a finishing touch, handstitch or hot-glue scraps of the variegated reembroidered lace on top of the flaps and then add buttons. Replace the original but-tons with decorative ones.

What to Use

Supplies: White knit cardigan sweater, Ecru #18 and Tan #16 RIT Dye, variegated re-embroidered lace in fall colors, Battenberg lace, clear hot-glue sticks, decorative buttons (optional), thread to match

Tools: Scissors, needle, hot-glue gun

Known as pointelle, the knitted lace on the hem and the cuffs of this sweater inspired me to choose these lacy embellishments.

Girlish Pinstripes

Add a little lace and your husband will probably never realize this *was* his jacket. If he doesn't have a coat to spare, comb thrift shops or discount stores to find some pinstripes just for you.

Remove all the buttons from the jacket and save them for a future project.

Cut two strips of ruffled lace trim, each equal in length to one lapel. Referring to the photo for placement, handstitch one strip to each lapel. To dress up the ruffled strips, add rose-patterned lace to the plain edges. Then stitch rose lace around the collar and at the top of each pocket opening.

Handstitch ribbon roses to the collar and to the pocket flaps (see the photos).

To finish, stitch gold-and-rhinestone buttons to the jacket front and to the cuffs. If you want to be able to button the jacket, you might need to widen the buttonholes, using a single-edged razor blade. Seal any frayed edges with liquid ravel preventer.

What to Use

Supplies: Man's pin-striped jacket, ruffled lace trim, rose-patterned lace, two colors of large silk ribbon roses, large gold buttons with rhinestones, thread to match, liquid ravel preventer (optional)

Tools: Scissors, needle, thimble, single-edged razor blade (optional)

Wide swaths of lace soften the sharp lines of peak lapels.

Monkey-on-My-Back Jacket

I am addicted to leopard spots, and the monkey on the back of my jacket is literally surrounded by them. You may have a craving for a fancy French tapestry or for one with cuddly kittens. Just pick a print that's "purrfect" for you.

This little monkey adds a whimsical touch to the back of my denim jacket.

Put the jacket on a flat surface. Lay tissue paper over the jacket. Trace patterns for the areas you have chosen to cover. Cut out the pattern pieces from the tapestry, adding ⅜" seam allowances to all sides. If your tapestry has a large motif, center the jacket's back pattern piece over it.

Turn under the ⅜" seam allowances on all the pieces and press. Pin the pieces in place on the jacket. Machine-stitch the pieces, using a straight stitch.

Choose two complementary braid trims. For this jacket, gold and black-and-gold trims were used. Hot-glue one trim along the side and the top of each front yoke piece, down the side of each pocket, and around the pocket flaps. Hot-glue the other trim down the sides of the gusset panels. Then frame the back panel—the focal point of the jacket—with a border of both braids.

Hot-glue a few Austrian crystals to the back jacket piece to highlight the tapestry designs.

Handstitch or hot-glue sequined and beaded appliqués to the front yoke and to the pocket flaps (see the photo on page 87). If you cannot find appliqués to suit your design, layer smaller appliqués together in a collage and hot-glue them in place. Embellish the appliqués by hot-gluing Austrian crystals on them. Stitch small beads in place on the appliqués as accents.

Hot-glue clusters of Austrian crystals in assorted colors to each stud down the jacket front and on the cuffs. Hot-glue ribbon roses on the studs on the pocket flaps. Handstitch beaded buttonhole appliqués over the existing buttonholes on the front and on the cuffs.

What to Use

Supplies: Blue denim jacket, tapestry fabric of your choice, beaded braid, woven braid, Austrian crystals in assorted colors, assorted sequined and beaded appliqués, small beads, ribbon roses, beaded buttonhole appliqués, thread to match, clear hot-glue sticks

Tools: Tissue paper, tracing pencil, scissors, straight pins, sewing machine, needle, thimble (optional), hot-glue gun

I used Austrian crystals to highlight the eyes, the fruit, and a few green leaves of my monkey-in-the-jungle scene.

Beaded Bags

These inexpensive purses are in practical colors: ivory, metallic gold, and black. And they're so easy—you can finish all three in less than half an hour.

Make sure that the outside of the purse is clean, especially if you are recycling an old purse.

To score the area that you plan to cover on the ivory purse, use sandpaper or embroidery scissors to roughen the area on the front flap so that the hot glue will adhere. Piece together scraps of various kinds of lace and use liquid ravel preventer to seal the raw edges. Arrange the pieces on the flap as desired and hot-glue them in place. Randomly hot-glue flat-backed pearls on the flap to complete the design.

Prepare the leather on the flap for the gold purse. Choose a scrap of pale gold lace. Hot-glue the lace to the front flap. Add a few beaded leaves and hot-glue them in place.

Score the leather on the flap for the black leather purse. Hot-glue a single lace appliqué with beaded fringe in the center of the flap, allowing the closure to still operate and the fringe to dangle.

Each of these purses is now a boutique-worthy bag that could sell for much more than it cost to make.

What to Use

Supplies: All-leather purse in desired color (new or old), lace scraps, beaded embellishments, liquid ravel preventer, flat-backed pearls, clear hot-glue sticks

Tools: Scissors, sandpaper or embroidery scissors, hot-glue gun

If you're going to make only one purse, go for the gold (center). It complements everything and can be used day or night in any season.

BombShell Bombers

One day when I had been appliquéing everything except the dog, my husband, Robert, came in and took off his black bomber jacket. I immediately started laying out beaded pieces of lace on it.

When Robert saw what was about to happen, he grabbed his jacket in horror and took me right out to buy my own leather bomber—a jacket that has turned out to be a mainstay in my wardrobe.

When Spencer and I are out looking for trouble, our beaded bombers help us keep our cool.

Score the leather where desired on the collar, the back, the shoulders, and the sleeves, following the directions on page 91.

Embellish the collar and the back of the bomber with lace scraps or complete appliqués. Then embellish the shoulders and the sleeves and put small beaded appliqués on the cuffs. Secure the edges of small pieces of lace with black puff paint. Glamorize the pocket openings by adding a few rosebuds here and there. Hot-glue black sequined roses on the studs.

What to Use

Supplies: Black leather jacket, lace scraps, reembroidered lace (Black is best, but RIT Dye comes in black, too.), black beaded appliqués, black puff paint, black satin rosebuds, black sequined roses, clear or black hot-glue sticks

Tools: Sandpaper or embroidery scissors, hot-glue gun

Your beaded bomber does not have to be as elaborate as ours. You can add elements to the design as you go along or change them. These jackets are constant works in progress.

Indian Summer Barn Jacket

Four pockets give you four chances to enhance with appliquéd fabric. I chose a gold floral jacquard that reminds me of antique upholstery.

Trace the pockets onto tissue paper, adding ¼" seam allowances. Cut them out from the gold floral fabric. Press under the seam allowances on all the pieces.

Machine-stitch or hot-glue the fabric to the pockets.

Cover the front placket with burgundy ribbon to capitalize on the contrast between the gold floral and the blue denim. If you want to button the jacket, slash openings for the studs, using a craft knife. Treat the edges with liquid ravel preventer.

Hot-glue the same burgundy ribbon to the pocket flap. Slash an opening for the stud and seal the edges with liquid ravel preventer. Button the flap down. Edge the collar and each of the pockets with gold braid or rickrack.

Cover the button forms with burgundy ribbon, following the manufacturer's instructions. Stitch one button on each of the pockets without a flap. Hot-glue a gold ribbon rose on top of each nonremovable stud on the placket, including the one on the pocket flap.

What to Use

Supplies: Denim duster with four pockets, wide burgundy brocade ribbon, gold fabric with sunflower design, gold braid or rickrack, button forms, gold ribbon roses, liquid ravel preventer, thread to match, clear hot-glue sticks

Tools: Tissue paper, sewing machine, scissors, hot-glue gun, craft knife, needle, thimble

This decorated jacket is now fancy enough to wear out for a night on the town.

Winter

All I want for Christmas is in this photograph.

What you see here are the only things I have ever asked for. My dearest wishes are fulfilled: a warm and cozy place, a whispered promise, anticipation, and my belief in winter's wonders, shared with my Santa, my New Year's date, and my only valentine.

Wrapped in Gold

For those golden moments, only an outfit this glittering will do. Elevate the status of a basic black jacket with gold trim. Embellish its perfect partner—a bustier—with more glitz, as well as lace and rhinestone buttons.

Gilded Bustier

To begin, choose the laces you will use. This bustier has black Chantilly lace reembroidered in gold, two tones of gold passementerie, two tones of gold Venice lace embellishments, and black lace with an unusual leaf design.

Place the lace scraps on the bustier to get an idea of how many layers it will take to make the underwear look more like outerwear. You can pin the embellishments in place while wearing the bustier or use a dress form, allowing for horizontal stretch (see Crystal Bustier on page 30).

Choose darker laces for the first layer and for the two back panels. Make sure you use a variety of tones for contrast. Keep your figure in mind when placing items: lighter areas will maximize, dark ones will minimize. Try going lighter on the bustline and darker at the waist for a slimming effect. Save the gold passementerie lace for the center of the bustier. You will be surprised at how easily you can achieve a gorgeous look.

Handstitch the lace pieces onto the garment when satisfied with the placement. Do not stitch across the stretch of the bustier. (You can also get good results using hot glue. The bustier will look the same, and no one but you will know your secret.)

Stitch copper braid at the back waistline to accent. Even though it won't be seen, it's a festive touch.

Hot-glue large gold buttons with rhinestones down the center front.

What to Use

Supplies: Ecru or white bustier, black Chantilly lace reembroidered in gold, two tones of gold passementerie lace, two tones of gold Venice lace embellishments, black lace with leaf design, thread to match, clear hot-glue sticks (optional), copper braid, large gold buttons with rhinestones

Tools: Straight pins, needle, thimble, hot-glue gun (optional), dress form (optional)

Holiday Tuxedo Jacket

Lay the appliqués on the jacket. Move them around or cut them as desired to suit your design. Cut the lace into the desired shapes.

Select beaded and sequined appliqués in two shades of gold for the pocket details. Place passementerie along the length of the jacket on both sides of the front opening. Add the beaded leaf appliqués at the top of each. Pin the appliqués securely to the jacket. Handstitch them in place. Put your needle into the jacket fabric first and come up in the appliqué. Use a thimble to work the needle through the lace.

Handstitch beaded appliqués to each lapel. Add beaded and sequined roses and leaves in a darker gold below the first appliqués.

Replace the front and cuff buttons with decorative gold buttons. Gold rose buttons with rhinestones look great. Use a large button at the front and two smaller matching buttons on the cuffs. If you have another large button, stitch it on the upper lapel to simulate a brooch. Add a gold beaded buttonhole appliqué to further enhance the design.

What to Use

Supplies: Man's black tuxedo jacket, assorted beaded and sequined appliqués in tones of gold, gold passementerie lace, decorative gold buttons, gold beaded buttonhole appliqué, thread to match

Tools: Scissors, straight pins, needle, thimble

Wear the bustier under the jacket in good taste. That way, it can be alluring and elegant at the same time.

Studded in Garnet

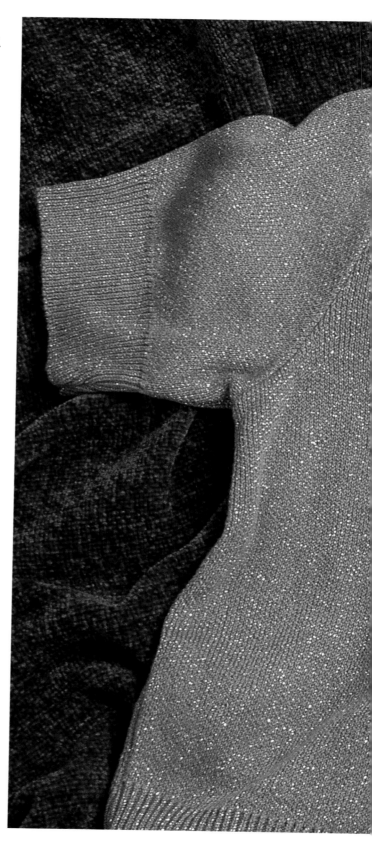

You'll be part of the party decorations when you walk in wearing this jeweled piece!

Dye the sweater in the washing machine, using Scarlet and a few drops of Wine, following the dyeing instructions on pages 122 and 123. (This was originally a white sweater with metallic thread running through it. The dye didn't color the metallic thread, so the sweater still has a glittery effect.) Lay the sweater flat to dry.

Center a sequined and beaded holiday appliqué at the front neckline and hot-glue it in place. Then attach red sequin florets in a staggered symmetrical pattern (see the photo).

Hot-glue flat-backed pearls around the red florets.

What to Use

Supplies: White cotton sweater with gold metallic thread; Scarlet #5 and Wine #10 RIT Dye; large red, green, gold, and fuchsia sequined and beaded appliqúe; red sequin florets; flat-backed pearls; clear hot-glue sticks

Tools: Washing machine, hot-glue gun

Mrs. Santa Claus Apron

If you're the woman of the house, chances are you are Mrs. Claus at Christmas. Why not play the day in costume?

Fold the apron in half lengthwise to find the center and press. From the top edge of the bib, measure down along the fold the width of the fur trim and mark, using a ballpoint pen. Measure up from the hem of the apron and mark the lower edge of Santa's jacket (the top of the bottom horizontal strip will align with this point). Unfold the apron.

Measure the distance between the two marks and cut a fur strip ½" longer than this measurement. Center the fur strip along the pressed fold and pin it in place, with ¼" at each end extending into the area that will later be covered by the horizontal fur trim pieces. Machine-stitch down the middle of the trim or hot-glue it in place.

These cookies were made and handpainted by "Lacy Lady" Carol Goodnight's mother, Inez. This year they will grace my Christmas tree as ornaments.

Measure the width of the apron at the bottom of the center fur strip. Using this measurement, cut a strip of fur trim to mark the lower edge of Santa's jacket. For a more finished look, cut the strip ½" too long to allow a ¼" turn-under at each end. Pin the fur strip in place, overlapping the center strip ¼". Machine-stitch or hot-glue the strip in place.

Cut fur trim for the top edge of the bib. For a neater look, miter the corners. Stitch the fur strip in place, overlapping the center fur strip ¼". Then cut one fur trim piece for each underarm curve, mitering the top corner of each to fit the top piece. Cut each strip at least 1" too long to allow for easing the trim around the curve and to provide a turn-under at the end.

Finish by handstitching or hot-gluing three large buttons down the center fur strip. Hot-glue your choice of Christmas decoration to a top corner or glue the decoration to a pin back if it cannot go through the washing machine. The rest of the apron is completely washable.

What to Use

Supplies: Red apron, white fur trim in desired width, thread to match, large buttons, Christmas decoration of your choice, pin and pin back (optional), clear hot-glue sticks (optional)

Tools: Ballpoint pen, straight pins, sewing machine, scissors, needle, thimble, ruler or measuring tape, hot-glue gun (optional)

Long Winter's Nap

Tired from fighting the Christmas crowds? Come home, kick off your shoes, shed those uncomfortable clothes, and slip into this cozy flannel nightshirt and slippers. Now pour some cocoa and curl up by the fire. Isn't that better?

Lace motifs turn a plain nightshirt into a seasonal pleaser.

Nightshirt

Remove the original buttons. Using a continuous piece of white picot trim, edge both sides of the front opening and the neckline. Handstitch or machine-stitch it in place with a straight stitch or a tight zigzag. Repeat to outline the side and bottom edges of the pocket.

Pin a piece of lace along the top edge of the pocket. Then tuck the top of a heart-shaped lace motif under it. Hot-glue them in place. Add a matching heart at the bottom of the front placket. Replace the original buttons with heart-shaped gold ones and then attach one to the pocket embellishments (see the photo). Stitch red ribbon rosebuds on the placket between the buttons and to the center of each heart-shaped motif.

Fold up the sleeves to form deep cuffs. Handstitch ecru and white appliqué pieces on the cuffs.

What to Use

Supplies: Man's plaid nightshirt, white picot trim, ecru and white lace embellishments, white heart-shaped lace motifs with black netting background, heart-shaped gold buttons, red satin ribbon rosebuds, thread to match, clear hot-glue sticks

Tools: Sewing machine, scissors, straight pins, hot-glue gun, needle, thimble

Slippers

Handstitch or hot-glue the picot trim across the cuffs (see the photo). Hot-glue a heart-shaped lace motif on each toe. Then add a red ribbon rosebud to the center of each heart.

This is a great beginner's project—perfect for a child to make. Use your creativity and fashion your own design, using pieces from other projects.

What to Use

Supplies: Red-and-plaid flannel slippers, white picot trim, white heart-shaped lace motifs with black netting background, red satin ribbon rosebuds, thread to match, clear hot-glue sticks

Tools: Scissors, hot-glue gun, needle, thimble

These plaid slippers will be ready in a flash for you to slip on.

Roses-in-the-Snow Shirt

Delicate passementerie lace and dusty pink ribbon roses work wonders for these wintry blues.

Make a collage of lace scraps for each pocket and top each with a ready-made beaded lace appliqué or two, using hot glue. Pin the lace pieces on the pockets and handstitch or hot-glue them in place.

Hot-glue buttons, flat-backed pearls, Austrian crystals, and ribbon roses on the pockets. (Be careful not to use too much glue or the pockets will be stiff and heavy.)

Embellish the collar as desired with lace scraps and buttons (see the photo).

What to Use

Supplies: Chambray shirt, assorted lace scraps, beaded lace appliqués, assorted buttons, flat-backed pearls, Austrian crystals in assorted colors, ribbon roses, clear hot-glue sticks, thread to match

Tools: Hot-glue gun, needle, thimble

The opalescent snaps on this shirt complemented my design so I decided not to change them.

Sweatshirt Chic

When I need to run errands but don't feel like dressing up, this sweatshirt still lets me show my style. By using your imagination and different colors of dyes, you could make one for every season.

Remove any labels on the outside of the sweatshirt. Dye the sweatshirt in a Moss Green dyebath with a small amount of Mint Green added to it (see the dyeing instructions on pages 122 and 123). Cut out pockets in the desired size from the rose brocade. Turn under a ⅜" seam allowance on each and press. Hot-glue brocade ribbon trim along the pocket tops. Embellish the lower edge of the pockets with ribbon lace trim left over from the Sunbathing Beauty Cover-up on page 52. Stitch one pocket in place on each side of the jacket.

Using one continuous piece, add brocade ribbon along each side of front opening and around the hood. Machine-stitch it in place.

Replace the rough cotton cord in the hood with a length of satin cording. Using a safety pin, attach one end of the new drawstring to one end of the old one. Draw the new cording through by pulling the old one out. To attach each tassel, pass one end of the rayon cording through the loop above the tassel. Make a loop and hot-glue the cording to itself.

Cut two rose motifs from the brocade. Treat the edges with liquid ravel preventer and glue or stitch them in place on one side.

What to Use

Supplies: White hooded sweatshirt, Moss Green #41 and Mint Green #8 RIT Dye, rose brocade, 1½"-wide brocade ribbon, ribbon lace trim, rayon satin cording, complementary tassels, thread to match, clear hot-glue sticks, liquid ravel preventer

Tools: Washing machine, scissors, straight pins, sewing machine, hot-glue gun, safety pin

I had teenagers in mind when I designed this project. A teen might wear this on a date or to a casual party. Grown-ups can make different versions of this sweatshirt as Christmas or birthday gifts.

Flower Finesse

When I make a corsage, I begin by shopping for my favorite materials. My most reliable haunts include crafts stores and bridal departments at fabric stores.

Spring

Summer

Fall

Winter

Bow Directions

Make a bow by pinching a loop of ribbon between your forefinger and thumb. This point is the center of the bow. Make another loop and pinch the ribbon again at the bow center. Then twist the ribbon one-half turn and make a second loop on the opposite side. Repeat to make a total of four to eight loops. Fold doubled florist's wire over the center of the bow and tightly twist the ends together.

Corsages

For the **Spring Corsage,** make a four-looped bow from pink satin wire-edged ribbon. Arrange flowers until you are satisfied with the color combination and the placement. Twist the wire stems together to form a mini bouquet. Add jeweled sprigs to frame the flowers. Fold the stem wires of the flower bouquet under (or trim them with wire cutters) and place the bouquet on top of the bow. Hot-glue the bouquet in place.

Add a bow of pearls-by-the-yard trim to elongate the design. To do this, make loops in various sizes with the pearl trim and wire them at the middle. Attach the bow by wiring it to the bottom of the bouquet. Glue the pin to the pin back. Let it dry. Hot-glue the corsage to the pin back. Let it dry, keeping the pearl strings free while the glue is still hot.

For the **Summer Corsage,** make an eight-looped bow from the rosebud ribbon.

Make a four-looped bow from wire-edged ribbon.

Hot-glue the beaded appliqués on top of the second bow. Wire the first bow to the center of the second bow, using florist's wire. Fill in the spaces between the appliqués and the rosebud ribbon with jeweled sprigs.

Hot-glue the pin to the pin back. Glue the corsage to the pin back. Let it dry.

For the **Fall Corsage,** make a four-looped bow from the burlap ribbon.

Fold a contrasting brocade ribbon scrap over and wire the ends together with florist's wire. Hot-glue the scrap to the center of the bow.

Arrange flowers as desired. Add jeweled sprigs that give the effect of berries. Randomly tuck the sprigs into the folds of the bow, hot-gluing each item as you add it.

Hot-glue the pin to the pin back. Hot-glue the corsage to the pin back. Let it dry.

For the **Winter Corsage,** make a four-looped bow from wire-edged holiday ribbon.

Nestle flowers in the center of the bow and hot-glue them in place.

To finish, hot-glue some jeweled sprigs among the flowers. Glue the pin to the pin back. Hot-glue the bow to the pin back. Let it dry.

What to Use

Supplies: Assorted wire-edged ribbons (or any wide ribbon), silk flowers with leaves, jeweled sprigs, pins and pin backs, pearls-by-the-yard trim, florist's wire, clear hot-glue sticks, narrow white satin rosebud ribbon, beaded lace leaf appliqués, burlap ribbon, brocade ribbon scrap

Tools: Scissors, hot-glue gun, wire cutters (optional)

Made-to-Match Jewelry

Porcelain Rose Earrings

Solve the problem of trying to find earrings and pins to coordinate with your outfits by making your own. Great-looking jewelry can be made from all kinds of materials. Try your hand at a little creating!

Porcelain Poppy Earrings

Easy Earrings

Wipe each metal earring back with acetone or nail polish remover to take off any finish and to improve the bond with the glue. Decide on an earring design. Working on one earring at a time, put jewelry cement on the earring back.

For each **Porcelain Rose Earring**, hot-glue the pastel porcelain roses on the earring back and then add a butterfly. Use a toothpick, if necessary, to move the pieces around until satisfied with the placement. Place the Austrian crystals last, using tweezers.

For the **Porcelain Poppy Earrings**, hot-glue porcelain leaves and poppies to circular earring backs (see the photo for placement). Add a clear Austrian crystal to the center of each flower and a green crystal to each leaf, using jewelry cement.

What to Use

Supplies: Earring backs; jewelry cement; porcelain roses in assorted colors; gold butterflies; topaz, green, and clear Austrian crystals; porcelain poppies and leaves

Tools: Acetone or nail polish remover, hot-glue gun, tweezers, toothpicks (optional)

Victorian Pin

To make a pin, hot-glue porcelain roses to a pin back, using jewelry cement. Hot-glue a jewelry finding to the back of the pin back (see the photo for placement). Add Austrian crystals around the edge of the pin back, using tweezers. Hot-glue the pin to the pin back.

What to Use

Supplies: Pin and pin back, jewelry cement, porcelain roses in assorted colors, jewelry finding, Austrian crystals, clear hot-glue sticks

Tools: Hot-glue gun, tweezers

Bewitching Black Bed Jacket

For snuggling up and reading on a long winter's night, nothing could be more cuddly than this former sweatshirt.

Fold an ordinary black sweatshirt in half down the front, matching the shoulder seams. Pin along the fold to mark the center. Cut along the center for the front opening, removing the pins as you work. Cut off and discard the ribbed neckband, creating a slightly bigger neckline. Then cut off and discard the ribbing at the waist and at the wrists.

Dip the large lace embellishments and the pearl-trimmed ribbon in a weak Cocoa Brown dyebath, just long enough to pick up a touch of color and to produce a romantic antiqued look (see the dyeing instructions on pages 122 and 123). Set them aside to dry.

Cut the pearl-trimmed satin ribbon in half lengthwise. Save one half for a future project. With the right side of the ribbon facing the fleece side of the jacket and the long raw edges aligned, pin the ribbon in one continuous piece along the sides of the front opening and along the neck edge, leaving ½" free at each cut end of ribbon and easing the fullness at the neckline. Fold the cut ends up even with the bottom edge of the jacket and pin them in place. Machine-stitch the ribbon to the jacket, removing the pins as you work. Fold the ribbon to the front of the jacket. Press the seam flat and then topstitch the ribbon in place.

Pin the large tinted lace pieces as desired along the neckline and down both sides of the front opening, placing adjacent edges under the ribbon. Crimp the ribbon along both sides

of the front opening as desired (see the photo). Hot-glue the ribbon in place at these points. Make a tuck to flatten the excess ribbon on each side of the neckline; hot-glue the tucks in place. Embellish the crimps and the tucks with silk roses. Hot-glue light brown satin rosebuds to the ribbon along the neckline and at each lower front edge. Then hot-glue a rosebud to the top of each tinted lace piece.

Slip ivory Venice lace leaves and champagne sequin embellishments under each ribbon rose and pin them in place until the desired effect is achieved. Then hot-glue or handstitch them to the jacket.

Hot-glue topaz Austrian crystals on top of the lace pieces.

Overlap the bottom edge of the jacket with the ivory lace trim, turning the cut ends under even with the jacket edges. Machine-stitch the lace in place with a narrow zigzag. Roll up the sleeves several narrow turns. Handstitch ivory lace trim to the top of the cuffs. Tack each cuff in place at the seam line.

What to Use

Supplies: Large or extra-large black sweatshirt, large ivory or white lace embellishments, approximately 2 yards of 3"-wide ivory satin ribbon with pearl trim, Cocoa Brown #20 RIT Dye, bronze silk roses, light brown satin ribbon rosebuds, ivory Venice lace embellishments, champagne sequin embellishments, ivory nylon-cotton lace trim, topaz Austrian crystals, thread to match, clear hot-glue sticks

Tools: Straight pins, scissors, sewing machine, hot-glue gun, needle, thimble

A friend who loves to read in bed asked me to make her a glamorous but comfy bed jacket. This one-size-fits-all sweatshirt did the trick.

Inspirations

Nothing sparks my creativity like a bargain.

Thrifty shopping will net deals galore. I frequent thrift stores and discount stores, often buying an item just for the fabric, the lace, or the buttons. Or I might buy a load of umbrellas on sale and save them to decorate for presents throughout the year.

I love buying off-season and try not to miss an after-Christmas sale—I load up on holiday decorations, ribbons, laces, and fabrics. Even if I don't know what to do with my treasures at the time, I save them; they'll prove to be the perfect additions to future projects.

Sequined leaf trim

Rosebud lace trim

Large gold sequined florets

Beaded fringe

V-shaped bridal lace appliqué

Silk ribbon roses

Sequined leaves

Black sequined lace

Sunflower

Small sequined florets

Ruffled lace

Sequined butterfly motif

Rhinestones-by-the-yard trim

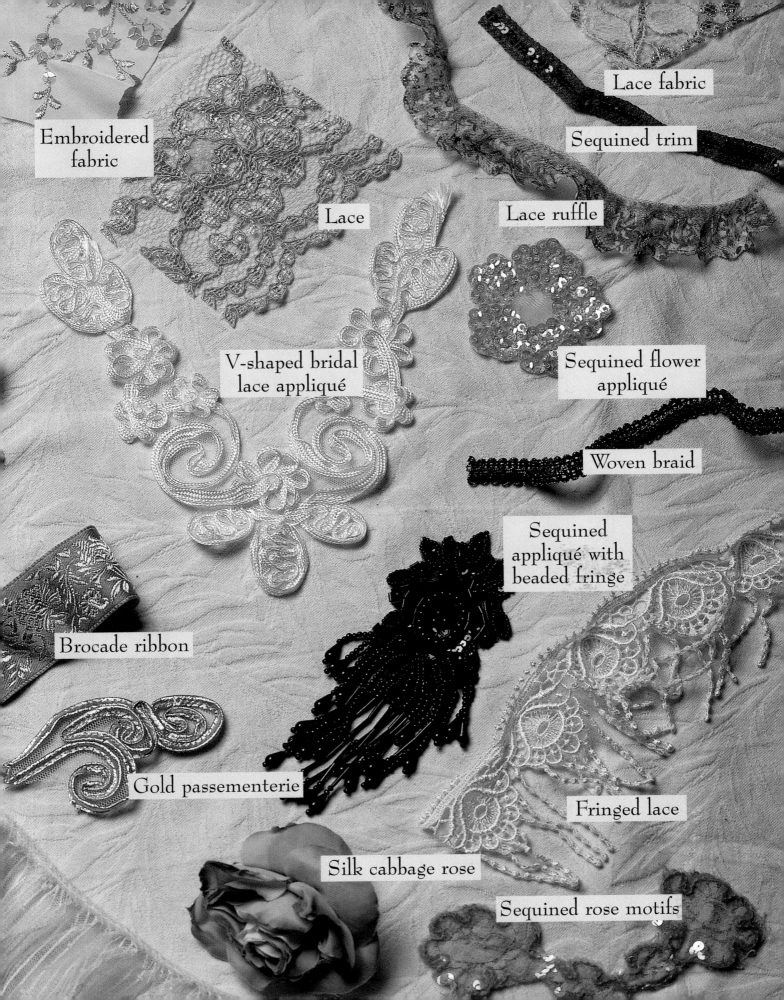

Lace fabric

Sequined trim

Embroidered fabric

Lace

Lace ruffle

V-shaped bridal lace appliqué

Sequined flower appliqué

Woven braid

Sequined appliqué with beaded fringe

Brocade ribbon

Gold passementerie

Silk cabbage rose

Fringed lace

Sequined rose motifs

Dyeing Instructions

Because I love to customize my clothes, I routinely dye plain garments. The process is simple and the end result is unique.

A newly purchased cloth garment may be stiff, making it hard to work with. If the item is washable, clean it in the washing machine and then dry it in the dryer with a fabric softener sheet. If the item is not washable, dyeing is not an option.

I recommend using liquid dye rather than powdered dye, because it is hard to get the powder to dissolve completely. However, powdered dye is concentrated, so if you want a strong or dark color, you may get better results with the powder. Follow the manufacturer's instructions for the first few projects until you are so familiar with the dyeing process that you feel confident to bend the rules (like I do!).

Experiment with colors. Mix as many colors as you want to get a pleasing color no one will be able to duplicate. Of course, this means that *you* can't duplicate it either, so dye everything that needs to be that color in the same dyebath. Because I like a variety of colors, I usually don't try to match the laces and the trims I am using on the garment. I just

I dyed the purse, the dress, and the matching shoes on pages 40 and 41 in the same dyebath. Stores can dye items for you, but it often takes several weeks. It's just as easy to obtain professional results at home.

make a note of the colors I used. If I need to add a piece of lace, I go for a complementary color or tone.

Mix up the dyebath just prior to use, either in the washing machine or in a large stockpot on the stove on high heat. Make sure the dyebath is thoroughly mixed before immersing any item. For the deepest color results, use the hottest water that is safe for your chosen item. The longer the item remains in the dyebath, the stronger the resulting color and the more colorfast it will be. Items can remain in the dyebath up to one hour (when the dye reaches its maximum strength) as long as the water remains hot and the items are frequently stirred or agitated.

Use rubber gloves to avoid staining your hands. Wear old clothes or slip on an apron to protect your clothing. If using powdered dye, wear a dust mask if possible. If not possible, open the pouch carefully just above the level of the water and pour the contents slowly to avoid dust.

Soak an item in plain, hot water until it is completely saturated before immersing it in the dyebath. Do not tightly bundle the garment, or it may end up with a tie-dyed effect. If your washing machine will agitate with the lid up, set the machine on the gentle cycle and keep it running as you immerse your chosen item. If the machine will not work with the lid up, immerse the item and close the lid for immediate agitation. When dyeing on the stove, continually swish the item with a wooden spoon. If any areas of the garment are exposed to the dye longer than the rest, an uneven color will result.

I usually dye items in a pastel color or dip them quickly in the dyebath to give a slight tint, to change the tone, or to get an antiqued

look. Remember, the longer you leave an item in the dye, the deeper the color will get until the dye has reached its maximum strength. Watch the dyeing process, stopping the machine now and then to check your garment. You might discover a color you love before the full strength of the dye has set in. (This is especially true when dyeing embellishments, such as lace or sequined appliqués.)

When dyeing beaded and sequined embellishments, remember that the thread that holds the beads and the sequins in place often dyes faster and darker. Also, light-colored sequins will absorb some of the dye. Natural fibers, such as cotton, rayon, and wool, will take the dye faster and stronger than some synthetic fibers, such as nylon and polyester. You can never be sure of the fiber content of laces and beaded pieces, so delightful color variations can result. Although different fabrics immersed in the same dyebath may dye in different tones, they will all have the same basic color and will blend well together. Keep these facts in mind when trying to dye items to match.

Rinse the dyed item thoroughly in cool or cold water. (Items from the same dyebath may be washed together in cold water, but do not wash them with regular laundry.) Hang it to dry.

To avoid an expensive accident with your regular laundry, *thoroughly clean your washing machine after dyeing.* Fill the machine with hot water, detergent, and bleach, and run through a complete wash cycle. Clean containers and sinks immediately after dyeing by scrubbing with hot water and powdered cleanser or bleach.

Hot-Glue Gun Tips

I keep a glass of ice water handy in case I accidentally get glue on my skin.

Apply a thin layer of glue to the underside of the lace.

Make sure that your supplies (hot-glue sticks, embellishments, and the items you are embellishing) are close at hand and that the hot-glue gun is heating up. (Let the glue-gun completely cool off before putting it away.)

Many of the steps in this book that require sewing can also be done with a hot-glue gun. Use your judgment when working on an item. If you take this shortcut, remember the following tips:

• Use a low-temperature hot-glue gun. Hotter glue may burn a hole in a delicate item, such as a nylon umbrella.

• Remember that clear hot glue shows up against a black background. Use black hot-glue sticks instead or cover up the edges of the excess glue with black puff paint.

• Cover the areas you are not working on, since it is difficult to get hot glue off a garment if you drip on it. Use an old towel, a cloth diaper, or a piece of scrap fabric.

• Control the temperature in your work area. Working in a cold area will shorten the time it takes for the glue to harden; working in a warm area will extend it.

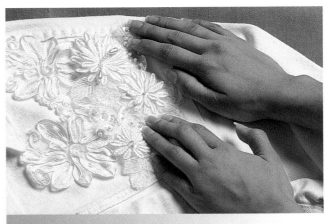

Press the lace in place and let it dry.

• Remove excess glue as quickly as possible if you accidentally apply too much. This can be done by remelting the glue with a blow dryer or the hot tip of the glue gun and then scraping and peeling.

• Make sure the surfaces of the items you plan to glue embellishments on are clean and free from oily film. Where necessary, I have made comments on surface preparation in the individual instructions.

• **Do not dry-clean any item in this book after you have embellished it using hot glue.** Dry cleaning can remove hot glue from a garment. Handwash or wash in the machine on the gentle cycle. Do not embellish with hot glue any item that is labeled "Dry Clean Only."

Sensible Stenciling

Use a stencil brush to evenly apply the paint.

Stenciling is an easy and fun way to decorate a plain item.

To make a stencil, trace the desired pattern onto the frosted side of a sheet of plastic template material. Place the plastic (shiny side up) on a protective mat. Cut out the stencil, using a craft knife.

Tape large pieces of waxed paper to the table or to the work surface. If desired, practice stenciling on muslin scraps before you begin your project.

Place the item to be stenciled on top of the waxed paper. Put the stencil where desired. Secure it with masking tape. Using a stencil brush and any stencil paint, stencil the pattern onto the item. Let it dry. Repeat as desired. (See Even Cowgirls Wear the Blues shirt and boots, pages 24–27.)

You can also trace a stencil onto the item and then fill in the design with puff paint (see Flowers 'n' Showers Umbrellas on pages 18–21). If you choose to trace the stencil, you can either outline the stencil with puff paint before filling it in or paint the stencil first and use the puff paint to cover up any rough edges. Apply the paint directly from the bottle and spread it with a paintbrush or a sponge.

Remove the stencil carefully so that the paint doesn't smear.

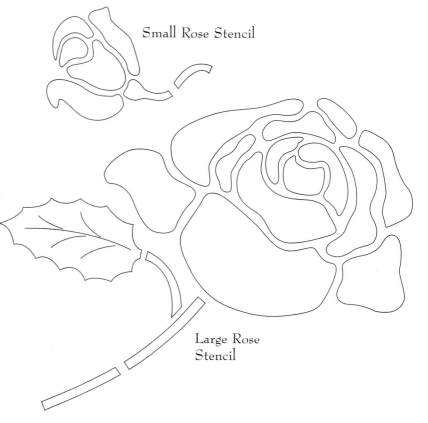

Small Rose Stencil

Large Rose Stencil

Index

Aprons
        Mrs. Santa Claus, 104–105
        Sweetheart, 16–17

Baby Rompers, Bodacious, 28–29
Barn Jacket, Indian Summer, 96–97
Bathing suit cover-up, 52–53
Bed jacket, 116–117
Belt Buckle, Summer, 60–61
Blouse, Flutterby Butterfly, 66–67
Bombers, BombShell, 92–95
Boots, stenciled, 24–25
Bustiers
        Crystal, 30–32
        Gilded, 100–101

Collars, Pet, 64–65
Corsages
        Fall, 112–113
        Spring, 112–113
        Summer, 112–113
        Winter, 112–113
Cover-up, Sunbathing Beauty, 52–53

Flip-flops, Froufrou, 56

Hair ornaments
        Blue Angel Bow Clip, 51
        Pretty-in-Pink, 51
        Ribbons & Roses Headband, 50
Hats
        Cranberry Chapeau, 78–79
        Meadow Flowers Sun Hat, 44–45
        Visor, Camellia-Kissed, 58–59
Headband, Ribbons & Roses, 50
Hightops, Forget-me-not Linen, 57

Peach Lacy Sweater, pages 46–47

Indian Summer Barn Jacket, 96–97

Jackets
        Barn, Indian Summer, 96–97
        Bed, 116–117
        BombShell Bombers, 92–95
        Girlish Pinstripes, 84–85
        Holiday Tuxedo, 101
        Jeweled Denim, 68, 70
        Monkey-on-My-Back, 86–89
        Sunflower Jeans, 36–37
        Tuxedo, 31–33
Jeans, Jazzy June, 48–49
Jewelry, Made-to-Match, 114–115

Nightshirt, Christmas, 106–107

Pet Collars, 64–65
Pumps, I-Could-Have-Danced-All-Night,
        40–41

Purses
    Beaded Bags, 90–91
    I-Could-Have-Danced-All-Night,
      40–41

Robe, Rosy, 34–35
Rompers, baby, 28–29

Shades, Swanky, 54–55
Shawl, In-the-Pink Fringed, 12–13
Shirts
    Roses-in-the-Snow, 108–109

Smashing Tennis, 58–59
stenciled, 24, 26–27
Shoes
    Forget-me-not Linen Hightops, 57
    Froufrou Flip-flops, 56
    Hightop Tennis Shoes, 68–69
    I-Could-Have-Danced-All-Night
      pumps, 40–41
    Light-on-Your-Feet Lace Sneakers,
      58–59
    Ruby Slippers, 62–65
Slippers
    Christmas, 106–107
    Ruby, 62–65
Sneakers, Light-on-Your-Feet Lace, 58–59
Sunglasses, 54–55
Sun Hat, Meadow Flowers, 44–45
Sweaters
    Peach Lacy, 46–47
    Pearls & Lace Cotton, 38–39
    Pointelle Perfection, 82–83
    Ribbons and Roses, 80–82
    Studded in Garnet, 102–103
Sweatshirt, hooded, 110–111
Sweatsuit, Absolutely Amethyst, 22–23

Tennis Shirt, Smashing, 58–59
Tennis Shoes, Hightop, 68–69
Tuxedo Jacket, 31–33

Umbrellas, Flowers 'n' Showers, 18–21

Vests
    Cabbage Roses, 76–77
    True Blue Denim & Damask, 14–15
    Victorian, 74–75
Visor, Camellia-Kissed, 58–59

Sunbathing Beauty Cover-up, pages 52–53
Swanky Shades, pages 54–55

Credits & Acknowledgments

My special thanks go to Danica d'Hondt, for talking me into doing this book, for focusing my vision, for writing a book proposal, and for delivering me to my perfect publisher.

Thanks to my helpful hands:

Trudy Reynolds, for shopping, schlepping, painting, sewing, and being my friend

Asik Petrossian, for precision sewing

Thanks to the makers of my magic:

Robin Rollins, for hair styling

Dana Jensen-Hiltunen, for makeup

Melanie Clarke, for assisting with the photo styling and for coordinating the New York fashion show

Ed Glaze, assistant photographer

Mark Gooch, freelance photographer

Spencer Rollins, for playing dress-up with me

Thanks also to the following:

Wendy Riche, my producer at "General Hospital," for allowing me the time to do this project

Kathy Jolie, for giving me my first bottle of fabric glue

All of my "Lacy Ladies" for their support

The town of Los Alamos, California, and Mattei's Tavern

All of my friends at Oxmoor House

And thanks especially to my husband, Robert, for putting up with months of my magic mess

Special Note

RIT Dye is a registered trademark of CPC International, Inc., Englewood Cliffs, New Jersey.